Kaija Saariaho

SEPT PAPILLONS

for solo cello

CHESTER MUSIC

This work was commissioned by the Rudolf Steiner Foundation. It is dedicated to Anssi Karttunen, who gave the first performance in Helsinki on 10th September 2000.

Duration: c. 11 minutes

Score available on sale: Order No. CH 62150

NOTATION

Trills should always be played up a semitone, unless otherwise specified.

————————⟶	change very gradually from one sound or one way of playing (etc.) to another.
⟩———o	diminuendo al niente
o——⟨	crescendo dal niente

All glissandi should be started at the beginning of the note value.

S.P.	sul ponticello
S.T.	sul tasto
N	normal (used with S.P. and S.T., otherwise ord.).
E.S.P.	estremamente sul ponticello: as close to the bridge as possible.
▽	add bow pressure to produce a distorted sound, in which the audible pitch is totally replaced by noise, then back to tone again.
° ⎸	natural harmonic
o ——————⟶ ⋄	move gradually from normal to harmonic sound (less and less pressure with the left hand).
tr∿∿ o (⋄)	a trill produced by alternating the finger pressure between normal (o) and light (harmonic, ⋄). The result should be alternating normal and harmonic sounds.

for Anssi Karttunen

SEPT PAPILLONS
for solo cello

Kaija Saariaho

Papillon I

Dolce, leggiero, libero

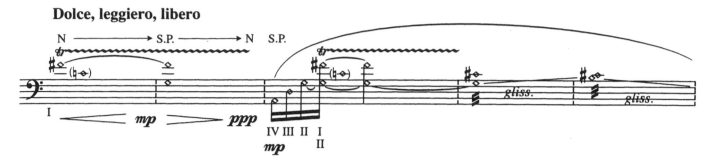

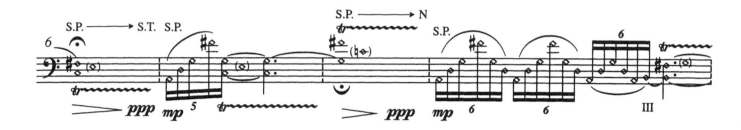

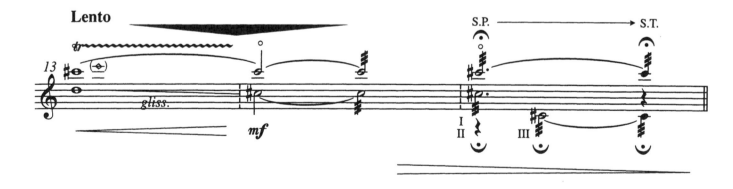

CH62150

Papillon II

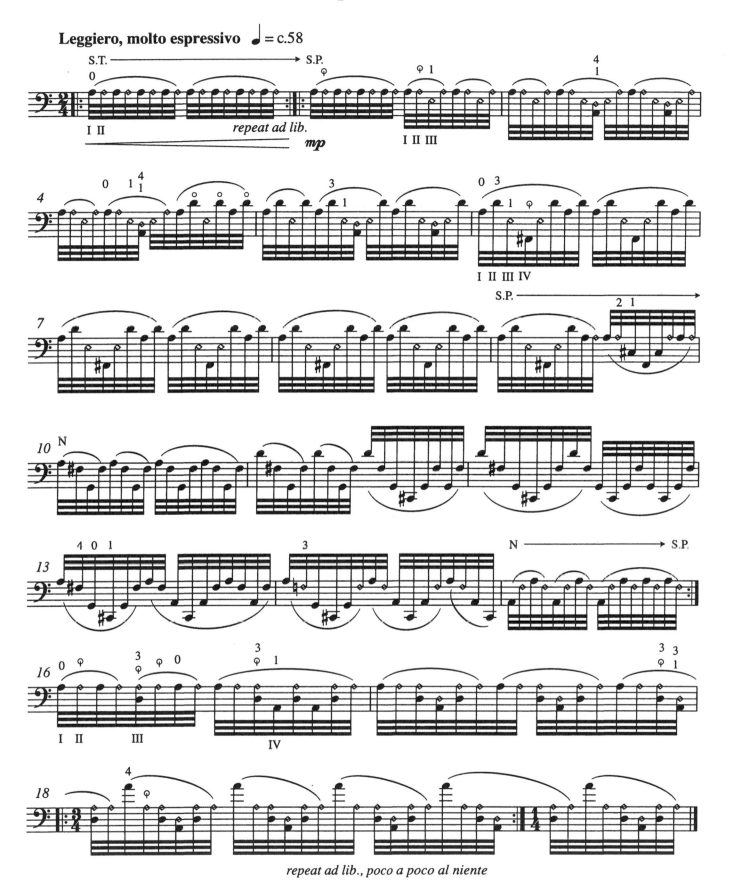

repeat ad lib., poco a poco al niente

Papillon III

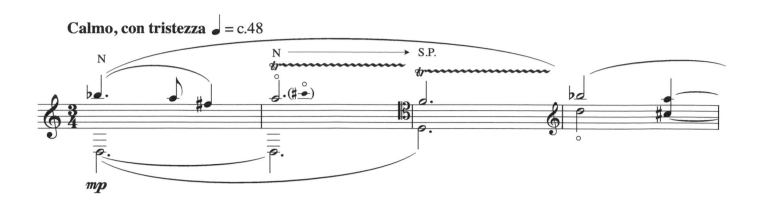

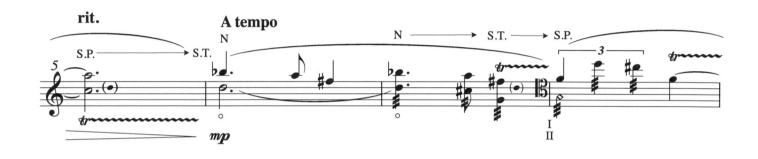

Papillon IV

Dolce, tranquillo

* None of the tremolandos in this movement is very fast. They may be played freely,
but always slowing the speed towards the end.

Papillon V

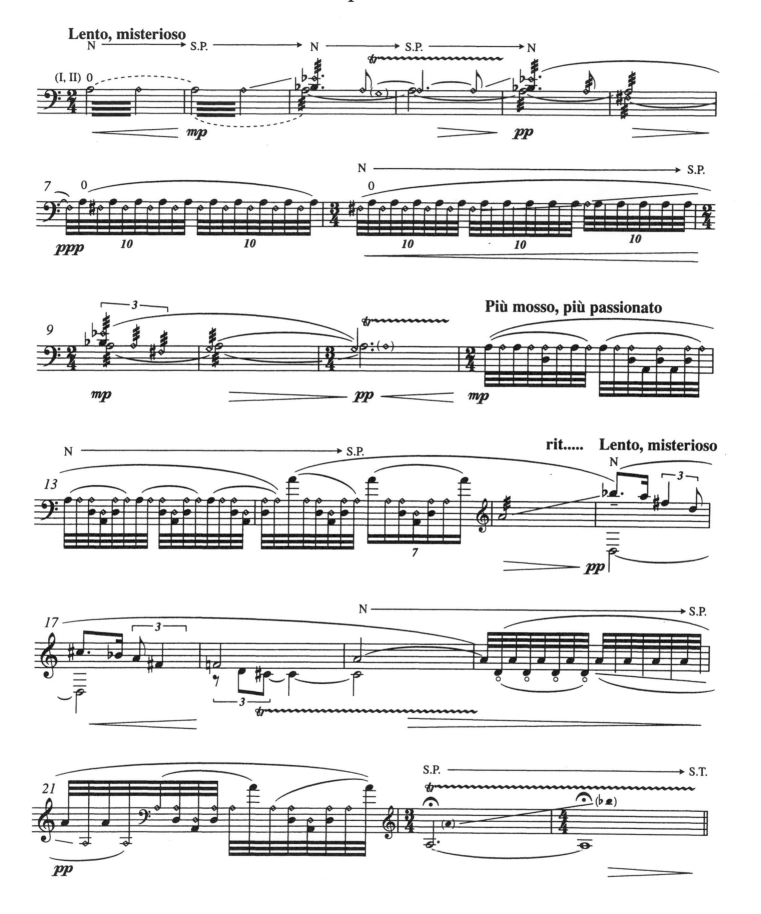

Papillon VI

Sempre poco nervoso, senza tempo (each 'bar' should last at least 5 seconds)

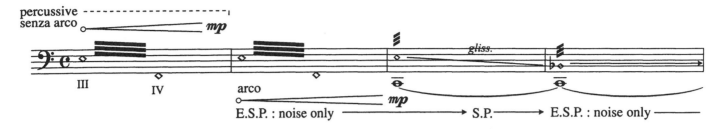

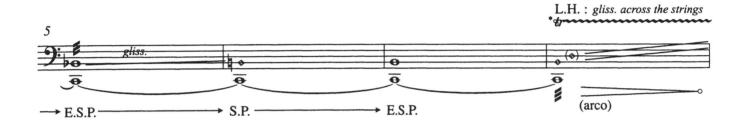

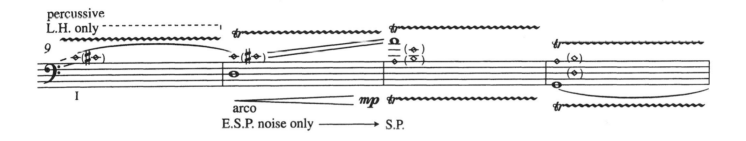

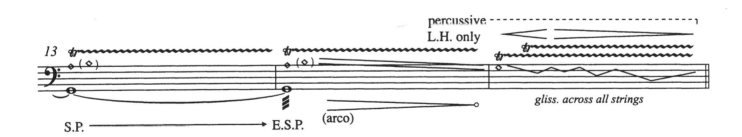

*In these harmonic trills, let the open strings resonate with the trills

Papillon VII